10.9°

CLEOPATRA
AND THE
EGYPTIANS

Andrew Langley

Illustrated by Gerry Wood

The Bookwright Press
New York · 1986

LIFE AND TIMES

Alexander the Great and the Greeks
Cleopatra and the Egyptians
Julius Caesar and the Romans
Alfred the Great and the Saxons
Canute and the Vikings
William the Conqueror and the Normans
Richard the Lionheart and the Crusades
Columbus and the Age of Exploration
Montezuma and the Aztecs
Elizabeth I and Tudor England
Atahuallpa and the Incas
Daniel Boone and the American West

Further titles are in preparation

First published in the United States in 1986 by
The Bookwright Press
387 Park Avenue South
New York, NY 10016

First published in 1985
Wayland (Publishers) Ltd
61 Western Road, Hove
East Sussex BN3 1JD, England

ISBN 0-531-18079-4

Library of Congress Catalog Card Number: 85-73586

Phototypeset by Planagraphic Typesetters Ltd
Printed in Italy by G. Canale & C.S.p.A., Turin

Contents

1 THE STORY OF CLEOPATRA

An Egyptian princess

Cleopatra VII was the last Queen of Egypt, but she was not an Egyptian. Her father, Ptolemy XII, was a Macedonian, one of a line of kings established by Alexander the Great after he had conquered Egypt in 332 B.C. For three hundred years, Macedonian and Greek soldiers struggled to keep the foreign rulers in power. But great discontent seethed just below the surface.

Thus, in 69 B.C., Cleopatra was born into an unhappy land, the remnants of a once-great empire. Egyptian influence had earlier extended south to Nubia and eastward to Syria and Lebanon, but after nearly three thousand years of independent power, she had been brought low. Wave after wave of attacks from her neighbors had culminated in the arrival of Alexander, and the country's pride was shattered forever.

When Cleopatra was still a child, another crisis struck. A force of native Egyptians, tired of foreign domination, expelled her father from the country. Unable to get any help from the Greeks, Ptolemy turned to Rome. This was a shrewd move, for Roman power was growing rapidly, and the ruling triumvirate gladly provided troops to restore the king to his throne. In this way, Egypt passed into the hands of a new master, becoming a monarchy protected by Rome.

In 51 B.C., Ptolemy died and his son became king, calling himself Ptolemy XIII. Cleopatra ruled with him. She was only eighteen years old, but she was soon to show that she was ambitious, bold and strong-willed.

Right *Cleopatra had a strong personality and she was ambitious. She dominated her weak brother in matters of state.*

Julius Caesar

It was not long before the headstrong Cleopatra clashed with her brother. Unlike other women of her time, she was eager to take part in the affairs of state, and was impatient of the King's weakness and lack of purpose. She was unscrupulous and single-minded in her ambition. She dreamed of restoring the dynasty of the Ptolemies to their former glory and of regaining control of lost territories such as Syria and the Lebanon. In addition, she wanted to share in the central power at Rome.

A civil war was the inevitable result of Cleopatra's differences with her brother, a war neither side was well enough equipped to win. Then, in 48 B.C., fate presented Cleopatra with a golden opportunity. Julius Caesar arrived in Alexandria in pursuit of his enemy Pompey. The

Caesar knew that it was in his interests to gain an alliance with the Queen of Egypt, but he also fell in love with her.

6

young queen seized her chance. Making use of her beauty and her intelligence she captivated the stern old warrior, pleading her cause against her brother.

Caesar certainly fell in love with Cleopatra, and indeed she is thought to have had a son by him. But being a wily politician himself, he realized that he could gain from an alliance with her. Closer contact with Egypt would give him access to that country's enormous wealth, which would help finance his own campaigns.

So he helped to defeat Cleopatra's opponents, including her brother, and restored her to the throne. In 46 B.C., now the undisputed ruler of Rome, he staged a triumphal procession through the city, proudly displaying his captives. Among them was Arsinoe, Cleopatra's younger sister, who had been hostile to her. Subsequently Arsinoe was set free and returned to the east, but in 41 B.C., Marc Antony put her to death, at Cleopatra's request. Cleopatra herself came to Rome, and from the autumn of 46 B.C. she lived in a sumptuous villa in the hills nearby, provided for her by Caesar.

Antony and Actium

The assassination of Julius Caesar in 44BC brought Cleopatra's life of ease to an abrupt end. She knew that the Roman people did not like or trust her, and so she made her way back to Egypt. It was not long, however, before another opportunity came her way in the shape of Mark Antony, one of the Roman leaders avenging the death of Caesar.

Arriving in Persia, Mark Antony sent for Cleopatra to ask her to give an account of her part in the recent wars between Caesar's supporters and Brutus and Cassius, Caesar's assassins. She made the grandest of entrances possible, sailing up the Cydnus River in a gorgeously decorated barge, dressed in cloth-of-gold and attended by musicians and pageboys. Mark Antony fell under her spell and became her lover.

Above *The Roman statesman Mark Antony.*

Above *Octavia, Mark Antony's wife and Octavian's sister.*

Right *After Caesar's assassination, Cleopatra slipped away from Rome and returned to Egypt.*

As a result of Caesar's death a power struggle had erupted between Mark Antony and Octavian, Caesar's great-nephew and heir. Antony eventually sailed to Rome and made a treaty with Octavian, sealing it by marrying his sister Octavia. But Cleopatra lured him back to her. He gave her control of valuable territories, such as Judaea and Arabia among many others and they lived in luxury together in the Egyptian capital.

In 33 B.C. Antony prepared for the inevitable war with Octavian. Octavian's fleet defeated the Egyptians and Mark Antony at the Battle of Actium in 31 B.C. Shortly after their defeat, and Octavian's occupation of Alexandria, both Antony and Cleopatra committed suicide. Before her death Cleopatra met with Octavian, probably to secure the safety of her children. Finally, she chose death by snake bite. She knew how significant this would be to the Egyptians because the snake was believed to be a minister of Amun, their sun god.

Above *Octavian, who later became the Emperor Augustus.*

2 THE LIFE-GIVING NILE

Farmers in the valley

Thousands of years ago the first settlers arrived on the fertile banks of the Nile.

In ancient times the prosperity, and security of Egypt were owed to the Nile River. Every spring, without fail, the river would swell up with the melted snow from the Ethiopian highlands in the south, surging down the Blue Nile. The banks would burst, flooding the surrounding land. A layer of fertile mud was left once the water had subsided. A damp, rich soil, warmed by the hot sun produced ideal growing conditions. This annual flooding was called Hapi, and was worshiped like a god. The people threw presents into the river in thanks for the fertility of the land and to ensure that there would be another flood the following year.

Thus the Nile created a narrow strip of magnificent

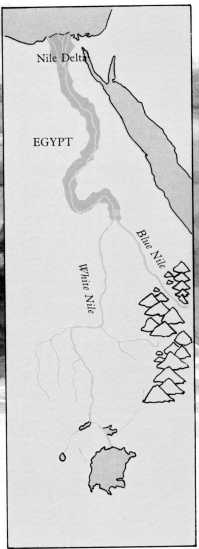

farmland, where as many as four different crops could be grown in succession each year. This strip ran the length of Egypt, fanning out into a delta at Cairo where it joined the Mediterranean. Beyond this fertile area lay desert. The desert and the unnavigable rapids of the river gave Egypt natural defenses against invasion and allowed the unmolested country to develop. Agriculture was the main occupation because the Nile provided an inexhaustibly fertile land.

The earliest settlers arrived there over 7,000 years ago. They soon fitted in with the simple and very regular pattern of the seasons. In July the floods came. In flood time the farmers worked on huge building projects during the reigns of the Pharaohs. In Autumn the crops were sown, irrigation ditches were dug and water was collected and kept. In March the drought began and the crops were harvested. With its natural riches, the valley seemed an almost perfect place to live.

Fertile area

Desert area

The Nile begins where the White Nile joins the Blue Nile. Without this river, Egypt would be a total desert.

A fragile paradise

The Nile provided these early farmers with many other things besides fertile land and a means of irrigation. The black river mud was used to make bricks and pottery. On the river's banks, in the marshy ground, papyrus reed grew. This had hundreds of uses. It could be lashed together in bundles to make boats, woven into mats and baskets, and beaten flat to make a kind of paper. The flowers of the plant were used for decoration. The river was also teeming with fish. The people fished in groups with large nets from the bank, or from reed boats.

The reeds gave shelter to many species of animals, including gazelle, wild duck and geese. The Egyptians hunted them with curved throwing sticks or with bows and arrows. The waters also contained more dangerous beasts, such as crocodiles and hippopotamuses.

But this paradise was never safe from disaster. When the Nile rose late or too little, then the crops would wither and famine would follow. When the floods came early or rose too high, then houses, people and animals might be swept away. Such calamities occurred at intervals during the three thousand years of the Egyptian Empire. The Egyptians did what they could to guard against lean years. They dug irrigation channels to take water to the fields when the river was at its normal level. When the water level was low the water that had been stored was directed down these channels. They also fixed gauges, which we call nilometers, at several points along the river's course. With these they could measure the height of the water and predict the probable rise of the river.

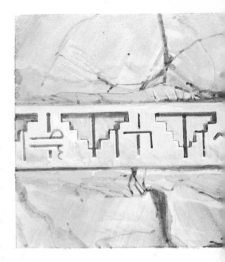

Above *This is part of the nilometer on the southern tip of Rodes, an island in the Nile near Cairo.*

Left *The early Egyptian settlers fought dangerous animals that lived in the waters of the Nile.*

Unification

The farming communities that settled along the banks of the Nile were among the earliest in the world's history. For countless thousands of years, people had wandered in bands, hunting and gathering whatever they happened to find. Now they could build permanent homes, herd animals and store food.

They lived in villages to provide protection against robbers. Farming was easy in the very fertile land and many people turned to crafts because there was no need for more farmers. They produced beautiful pottery and carvings in bone and ivory. They chipped out vessels in amazing shapes, from flint and other hard stones. This was

Left *Egypt, before the first Pharaohs, was divided into two regions, Upper and Lower Egypt.*

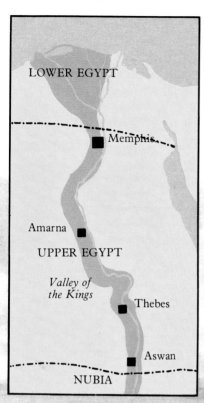

very difficult with the tools available. Trade with other countries began to flourish and precious metals were shipped up the Nile.

All that was lacking was unity. The different tribes of the Nile Valley each had its own leaders, its own religion and its own ways of farming. Gradually, as one tribe conquered another, the groupings became larger. By about 3200 B.C., there were two rival areas — Upper Egypt and Lower Egypt.

Little is known for certain of these very distant events in Egyptian history. It is believed that Lower Egypt was overcome by the armies of Upper Egypt, and that the two regions were unified for the first time. The king of Upper Egypt was called Narmer. He was the first Pharaoh and ruler of the unified country. He wore two crowns to show that he was ruler of both lands, and built a palace at Memphis, which lay on the boundary between the two regions.

Below *The settlers on the banks of the Nile built villages with walls around them to protect them from attack by robbers.*

3 EGYPT UNDER THE PHARAOHS

The Old Kingdom

Below *The Egyptians had to import lumber, which was brought in fleets of ships from the Lebanon.*

The unification of the country marked the beginning of the rule of the Royal Dynasties. Over the next 3,000 years they were to rise and fall. Sometimes drought brought famine and chaos; sometimes the monarchy grew weak and civil war flared up; sometimes foreign invaders took control. Yet these periods of misery were matched by periods of dazzling greatness, which produced the most magnificent monuments of any civilization.

The first great age of Egypt was called the Old Kingdom, which dated from 2686 B.C. until 2180 B.C. It was during this period that the great pyramids were built

using stone quarried from the banks of the Delta and the granite cliffs of Aswan. King Zoser was buried beneath the mighty Step Pyramid at Saqqara, overlooking the Nile. The names of Snefru and Cheops are famous today, not because of their deeds, but because of their vast memorials. The first true pyramid was built for Snefru, but the best-known are the two huge monuments at Giza. They cover the tombs of Cheops and his son Chephren, who also commissioned the carving of the Sphinx.

Egypt grew in prosperity and power. Expeditions were sent to subdue the marauding Nubians in the south, and to open up trade routes. The Egyptians badly needed lumber, because the palm or acacia trees which grew in Egypt did not provide good quality lumber. The country we know as Lebanon grew great cedar trees which were exported to Egypt. One fleet alone is recorded as consisting of forty vessels, each crammed full with huge trunks of cedar.

Above *The ancient Step-Pyramid at Saqqara — one of the oldest buildings in the world.*

The Pharaohs took part in daily religious ceremonies, giving offerings to the gods.

Pharaoh — God on earth

During the period of the Old Kingdom, the power of the king grew enormously. The Egyptians believed that Narmer, the unifier of the country, was a descendant of the gods. Therefore all the kings who followed him were also gods, who alone could protect their people. They made laws, and their every word had to be obeyed. They led their armies in battle, and they communed with the gods, and their ancestors, in splendid temples, praying to them for peace and prosperity. They traveled around their kingdom on a perpetual royal progress, inspecting farmlands, irrigation systems and new building projects.

The kings could not be referred to directly by name or title, because of their exalted position. So, people referred to the "great house," or palace, instead, which was pronounced "per-o" in the Egyptian language. This is where Pharaoh comes from.

18

The Pharaohs used to wear a double crown — the Red Crown of Lower Egypt and the White Crown of Upper Egypt — as a constant reminder that Egypt had once been two countries. They carried a crook and a flail, which were symbols of their authority, and they wore false beards as a sign of masculine power.

As a Pharaoh was a god he could not take a mortal woman to be his queen. It became the custom therefore for Pharaohs to marry women with their blood, such as their sisters of half-sisters.

A Pharaoh's life was strictly ordered. He had absolute power but the day-to-day running of the country was seen to by an army of ministers and officials, the most important of whom was his vizier. The most famous of these viziers was Zoser's vizier, Imhotep, who supervised the building of the Step Pyramid. Imhotep was also a notable physician, astronomer and magician. After his death he was revered as a god.

Below *A statue of Imhotep, King Zoser's vizier.*

19

The Middle Kingdom

The mystery and authority of a Pharaoh lasted only as long as he was successful. When crops failed, or battles were lost, the people soon began to panic. As the Old Kingdom came to a close, increasing power fell into the hands of the local governors, or nomarchs. Records show that there was widespread unrest, as civil war split the land. This was largely due to a prolonged drought, when for several years the Nile failed to rise to the normal flood level. The resulting famine was so severe that, in parts of Upper Egypt, people are thought to have resorted to eating each other.

In about 2133 B.C. the country was united by Theban princes who founded the Middle Kingdom, which lasted until 1633 B.C. It was a period of great prosperity in Egypt, under the rule of strong kings. These rulers left

Right *A nomarch was a powerful local governor during the Middle Kingdom.*

nothing behind them as magnificent as the Great Pyramids. They chose to be buried beneath much smaller pyramids, many of which have since crumbled away. But these new rulers brought stability. The nomarchs were subdued, and trade was resumed with Lebanon and countries to the east.

Egypt's defenses were strengthened, too. A massive fortress was built on the Libyan border, and others in Nubia. A line of strongholds, called "The Walls of the Rulers," guarded against attacks from Asia. Even this could not last forever, and at the close of the Thirteenth Dynasty, Egypt suffered the shame of being invaded. From the east came the Hyksos, who took control of Lower Egypt.

During the Middle Kingdom Egypt's defenses were strengthened, in part, by building a huge fortress on the border with Nubia.

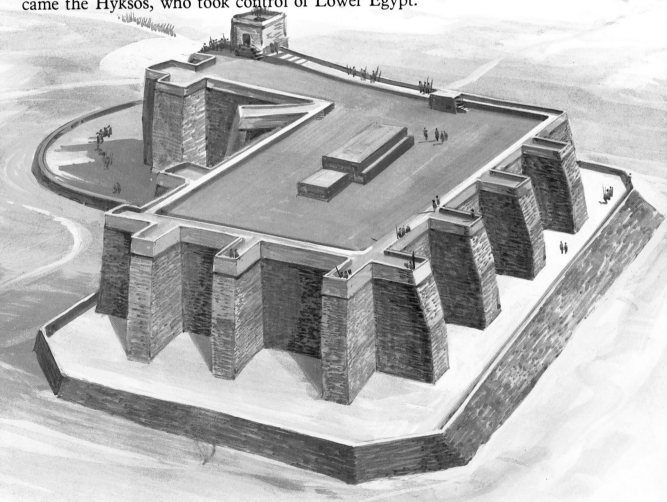

The New Kingdom

The invading Hyksos were eventually driven out of Egypt after 100 years of occupation.

The Hyksos, or shepherd kings, were eventually driven into southern Asia in about 1567 B.C., and the new Theban dynasty set about the task of expanding the power of the nation. This was the beginning of Egypt's most powerful age, known as the New Kingdom. Riches began to pour into the country. Many vast and complex temples were built, and the first of the magnificent tombs were constructed in the Valleys of the Kings.

Princess Hatshepsut was the first ruler of this period. She was married to the heir to the throne, Tuthmosis II. He died young and was succeeded by his son; but Hatshepsut pushed him aside and became Pharaoh herself. This was extraordinary in a country where, although women had great influence, only men could rule.

Tuthmosis III succeeded her. He was Hatshepsut's stepson-nephew and had long resented her position. When she died he went through her temple throwing over the statues as a mark of his angry feelings against her. He was Egypt's greatest warrior Pharaoh. He pushed Egypt's frontier as far as the Euphrates River. He led many expeditions into Palestine and Syria, and established control of Nubia once again.

When Akhenaten came to the throne in 1367 B.C. he neglected foreign affairs, concentrating instead on an attempt to impose a single religion upon his people. His suppression of the cult of Amun — the sun god — and his worship of Aten brought Egypt to the brink of civil war again. Sensing weakness, the Hittites from the east began to invade the Empire. Only the determined warfare of later Pharaohs, such as Seti I and Rameses II, kept the Egyptian frontiers safe.

Above *Princess Hatshepsut, the first ruler of the New Kingdom.*

Above *Tuthmosis III, a great warrior King.*

23

Above *Akhenaten had little time for affairs of state while he was Pharaoh.*

Below *Akhenaten and his Queen, Nefertiti, worship the sun god Aten with their daughters.*

4 GODS AND PRIESTS

Cult of the sun

The Ancient Egyptians saw their world in a very different way from us. At the center of it was Egypt herself, a flat disk floating upon the waters of Nun, the underworld. The Nile River flowed from this life-giving ocean, and the sun rose out of it each morning, to be pushed across the sky by a scarab beetle as though it were a ball of dung. Fixed like a roof above were the heavens, supported by four pillars.

This world was watched over by a complex race of gods. They varied from region to region and, over the many centuries, changed their names and roles.

Sometimes, these gods were merged into each other. They were the most important aspect of Egyptian life and they took human shape in the form of the Pharaohs.

The earliest god of the Old Kingdom was Atum, "The Complete One," who later became merged with Ra, the sun god. In the underworld dwelt Osiris, who gave new life to the land, and who judged the souls of the dead.

When Memphis became Egypt's chief city, its local god Ptah was regarded as the creator of all things. With the rise of Thebes to chief city came the rise of Amun, who was also identified with Ra. Akhenaten, as we have seen, tried to replace all these different gods with the worship of a single god, Aten. It was a brave attempt to bring unity to Egyptian religion, but stirred up such passions that it was doomed to failure.

Above *The god Ptah, the protector of craftsmen, and founder of Memphis.*

Left *A statue of the three gods, Horus, with his falcon's head, Osiris, god of the dead, and Isis.*

25

The inner shrine

A high priest in his leopard skin cloak.

Each god had his own temple. Depending on his importance, this might be a small brick building or a vast system of courtyards and halls, such as the temple of Amun at Karnak. The courtyards were open to all, but the central shrine could only be entered by a king, or by the priests who represented him.

The Pharaoh was the high priest of all the temples of Egypt. The vizier, and other prophets and officials closest to the king, were the senior priests. Below them were ordinary priests who took part in the religious ceremonies every day throughout the land. The priestesses provided music, on sistrums, which were like metal rattles.

The daily ritual was of great importance. It reminded the people of the power of the gods and the king. Each morning and evening the High Priest, wearing his ceremonial cloak of leopard skin, broke the seals on the door of the inner shrine. Inside was the image of the god, usually a small statue of gold or bronze. The god was greeted with hymns and prayers, and the statue was washed, oiled and dressed in fine cloth. An offering of food and drink was laid before it, to give the god energy for the new day. It was believed that the gods needed food and drink to nourish them, just as human beings did. Then the priests withdrew, and the doors were sealed up again. The ordinary people had their chance to see the image when it was paraded through the streets during festivals. There were many of these each year, some lasting for several days.

Right *The enormous, columned hall of the Temple at Karnak dedicated to Amun-Ra, the greatest god of the New Kingdom.*

Life after death

Below *A mummy from the eighteenth dynasty.*

The Egyptians firmly believed that death was the beginning of an eternal life. The spirits of the dead were attached to the corpse and would live on in the tomb, watching over the land. The most important spirits, of course, were those of the Pharaohs, because they were thought to be descended from the sun god. It was believed that as the king sat on the throne the spirit of the god Horus entered him. When he died, he immediately became one with Osiris, the god of the dead.

The Pharaohs' tombs were very grand, and a king often spent a large part of his reign supervising the building of his tomb. During the Old and Middle Kingdoms, the Pharaohs were buried beneath vast pyramids, with their chief officials buried near them in much smaller tombs, called *mastabas*. During the New Kingdom, however, the first royal tombs were constructed in a rocky area near Thebes. In the centuries that followed, every Egyptian king was buried there in an elaborate tomb, and today it is known as the Valley of the Kings.

Before burial, the body had to be carefully prepared for the afterlife. The Egyptians believed it had to be kept as complete as possible to allow the soul to return to it. In a long ceremony, the brain and other organs were cut out. The body was dried completely, stuffed with linen and spices, and anointed with preserving oils and ointments. Then it was wrapped up in many yards of linen bandages. The corpses of ordinary people were placed in simple graves. But those of kings and high priests were sealed in splendid coffins. The walls of the tombs were painted with pictures of the world outside, and food, drink and other goods were left beside the coffin. Instructions were left on papyrus scrolls in the tomb, to help the dead on their journey by giving them a route to follow and spells to protect them. The journey ended with the final judgment when the heart of the dead person was weighed, by the god of Anubis, on a scale against the Feather of Truth. A heart that was heavy with wickedness signaled a dreadful fate for its owner.

Above *The funeral procession for a Pharaoh was a grand occasion. The Pharaoh's organs were carried ahead of the mummified body.*

Right *A mudbrick house which was placed inside a tomb, representing a home in this world, and providing a home for the soul in the next world.*

5 EGYPTIAN BUILDING

Wonders of the World

Of the Seven Wonders of the Ancient World, the Pyramids are the only ones to have survived. Their size alone is staggering enough: the Great Pyramid at Giza is 230 meters (252 yards) long on each side, and contains over 2,300,000 blocks of stone, weighing an average of 2½ tons each. It is built with extraordinary accuracy. The four sides differ by no more than 20 cm (8 inches) in their lengths, and the right angles at the corners are almost exact.

Yet the Egyptians had no cranes, no pulleys, no scaffolding and not even any wheeled cars, let alone the vast machines used in big building projects today. Their only tools were simple — wooden squares, plumb lines and

Above *A stonemason's wooden mallet.*

Below *Carpenters tools: 1 Ax; 2 Saws; 3 and 9 Adze; 4 Bowdrill; 5, 6, 7 Bradawls; 8 Chisel; 10 Oil holder; 11 Honing stone.*

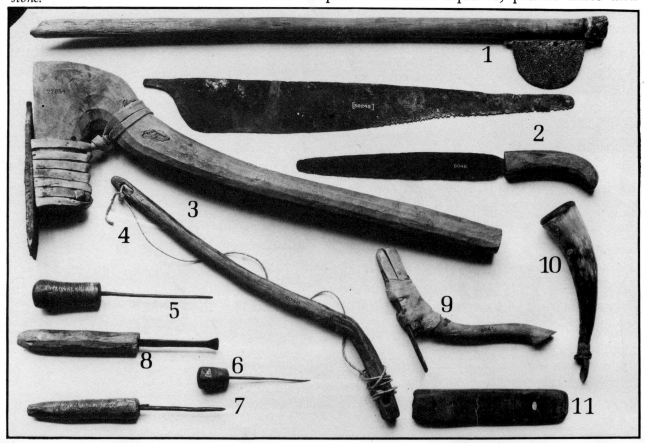

stone hammers. What made all this endeavor possible was the enormous amount of muscle power available. Hundreds of thousands of men were idle each year during the months of the flood, and so they were recruited as building laborers.

The stone came from quarries near the Nile. The blocks were hacked out with hammer and chisel and hauled on sledges or rollers down to the river. Rafts took them to the building site, where they were again hauled into position and smoothed off. But how were the blocks raised onto the walls? The men piled up sand and rubble, making embankments up which the stone could be pulled. As the pyramid grew higher, the rubble was heaped higher too. When the building was complete, the banks were simply dug away again.

Below *Hundreds of men worked hard to pull blocks of stone up the rubble embankments to build the pyramids.*

6 EVERYDAY LIFE

Part of a vizier's work was to listen to appeals from the people.

Government and the Law

The organization of Egyptian society was so strong that it remained very stable over long periods. Even after times of civil war and chaos, much the same system of government would be set up. At the top, of course, was the Pharaoh. Around him were courtiers and other officials, of whom the vizier was the most important. Every day the vizier would attend the king for instructions and to tell him of the affairs of the country. Then he would go to his offices and spend long hours reading documents, hearing appeals and planning expeditions or building projects.

The vizier was probably the busiest man in the land.

Beside his office work, he would often take the king's place on the tours of inspection during which he checked irrigation channels, levied troops and counted herds of cattle. It was his job, too, to measure the rising of the floods by looking at the nilometers.

Egypt was divided into forty-two regions, or nomes, each of which had a governor chosen by the king. It was these nomarchs, as they were called, who had rebelled to cause the downfall of the Old Kingdom. The larger towns were governed by mayors, who were also tax officials. Being a tax collector was an unpopular job. They had to punish those people who avoided tax by beating them until they paid up. The tax was not collected in money but in food, livestock or goods which had to be stored safely until it was demanded by the vizier. If any disaster occurred to the farmer's crops, the tax officials did not reduce their demands.

Below *A taxman takes away part of a farmer's flock of geese, as his tax payment.*

The tombs in the Valley of the Kings were discovered by thieves and robbed. The bodies of the kings were often destroyed.

The secret tombs

The pyramids, with their royal ghosts and sumptuous grave goods, remained sealed up for many centuries. But eventually their magic faded, and thieves broke in to ransack the treasure.

During the New Kingdom, Tuthmosis I decided that he should be buried in a more secret spot. He chose a remote valley near Thebes on the west bank of the Nile, above which there loomed a pyramid-shaped cliff. Instead of erecting a memorial, he had his tomb dug deep down into the valley, with the entrance carefully hidden. Over the next five centuries, all the Egyptian kings were buried there. They did their best to keep the secret by using only workmen from the nearby village of Deir el Medina. The inhabitants were ordered not to speak of the graves, and all their food and water was supplied by the state.

The later tombs are some of the largest and most complicated of man-made caverns. From the massive entrances, long passages sloped down underground. The walls were covered in richly colored paintings and relief sculptures with many false doors and pits to confuse would-be robbers. The burial chambers were filled with precious objects such as beautiful clothes and perfumes, statues and weapons plated with gold and carvings made from alabaster.

For all their careful planning, alas, the Pharaohs could not keep their secret forever. In the end the robbers found their tombs, stole what they could sell and smashed the rest. Tutankhamun's tomb survived total desecration, although there were certainly two raids carried out on it. During one of these attacks the robbers must have been disturbed, as a bag of gold rings was found abandoned.

Below *The tomb of Seti I, of the nineteenth Dynasty. It was dug 213 meters (700 feet) deep into the rock in the Valley of the Kings.*

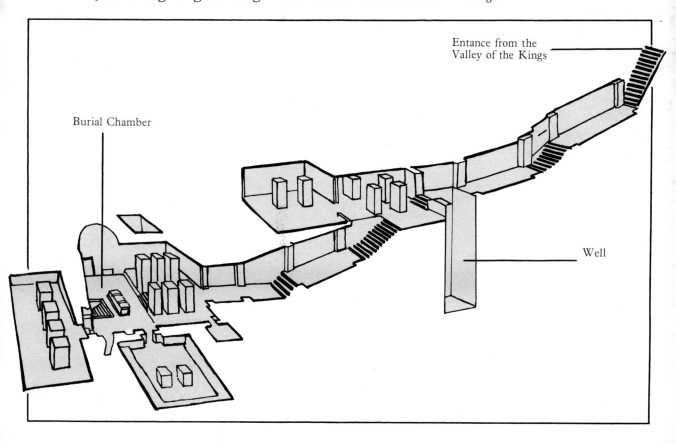

Entance from the Valley of the Kings

Burial Chamber

Well

Above *The farmers would plow the fields once the flood had subsided.*

Below *A wooden hand plow.*

Food and wine

The most important crops for the Egyptians were barley and wheat. As soon as the annual floods had receded, men would move across the black-silted fields clearing away weeds and breaking up the packed soil with hoes. Plows pulled by oxen and donkeys would gouge out furrows, and behind them would walk the sowers, scattering seed by hand. Sheep or pigs would later be driven over the fields to trample the seed into the ground.

While the crops were growing, they were measured by the tax officials, who decided how much each farmer would have to pay. Then came the harvest. The cut grain would be spread out on the ground and trodden on by oxen to break off the husks. These would be removed by winnowing — tossing the grain in the air with wooden spades so that the husks blew away.

Grain was stored in silos made of brick, and was used for making the two great staples of the Egyptian diet —

bread and beer. Together with vegetables such as onions, leeks and lettuce, these were all that the common people could afford to eat. Their meat came from large herds of cattle, sheep and goats. A large number of the cattle were actually used for sacrifices at the temples and tombs, and ended up being eaten by the priests. However, priests were forbidden to eat pork, so ordinary folk made the most of their pigs.

The Egyptians also grew figs, dates, pomegranates and grapes. They took great care with their fig trees and date palms, and built elaborate wooden trellises for their vines. The grapes were trampled to make wine, which was stored in clay jars.

Above *A wooden model of a figure grinding corn, which was discovered in a tomb.*

Below *The farmers used shadufs for moving water in the fields from one level to another.*

Craftsmen and scribes

The fertility of the Nile Valley brought prosperity to Egypt. This in turn allowed craftsmen and artists to flourish. Over the centuries they developed astonishing skills, using the simplest of tools and materials. Some made things to be sold locally, other were employed by wealthy patrons in their own workshops. These men were paid with food and clothing instead of money. The craftsmen who worked on the Pharaohs' tombs in the Valley of the Kings were sometimes rewarded with wine or meat.

The most plentiful materials were clay and stone. Egypt was rich in ornamental stone. Clay was used to make everyday objects, such as bowls and cups, but stone had more care lavished upon it. It was first used in building as part of the decoration. It must have taken enormous patience to carve vessels from hard stone, like alabaster.

Carpenters had to rely on wood imported from Phoenicia and Lebanon. With it they made everything from household furniture to river boats. Their most

Egyptian life was recorded by scribes on papyrus scrolls. They usually sat cross-legged when they worked and used reeds to write with.

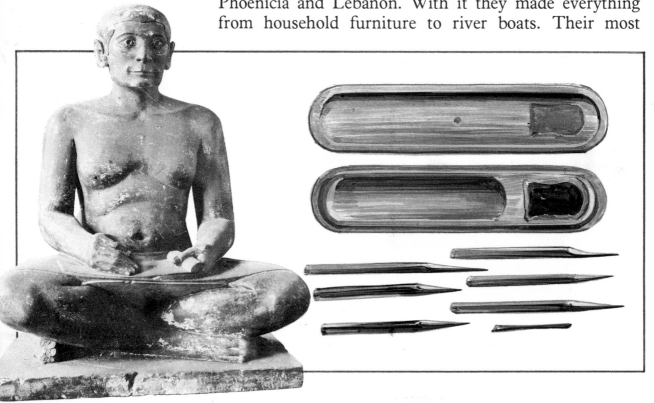

important work was the carving of statues of gods for the temples. These were often covered in gold leaf.

Artists were employed to decorate the walls of tombs and temples with paintings of the next world which could come alive for the spirits of the dead. The colors of the paints were made from minerals, which were ground on stone pallets and mixed with water. Glue or egg was added to act as an adhesive. The paint brushes were usually sticks of fibrous wood which had been soaked in water. For fine work the tips of rushes were used.

Egyptian history was written down on papyrus scrolls by scribes. Instead of letters they used hieroglyphs, a system of symbols which carried different sounds. Learning to write must have been a hard task because there are known to have been at least 800 different symbols.

The sculptors worked on the enormous tombs of the Pharaohs in teams, taking a day off every ten days.

A farmer's house was quite simple and built on two levels. In order to keep cool, the family would spend most of their time on the upper level.

Life at home

As in any country and any age, there was an immense difference between the lives of rich and poor. Noblemen and wealthy officials could afford to build large villas in the countryside, where there was room for gardens and outbuildings. The garden might have a fish pond, an orchard and a small family temple. These villas were often beautifully decorated inside, with friezes painted around the walls, sometimes of brightly colored flower designs. The ceilings were high, supported by plastered, wooden pillars. The furniture was made of the finest wood the owner could afford, such as ebony or cedar. This class of family slept on beds, which was a mark of their position, distinguishing them from peasants and nomads.

Skilled workers usually lived in terraces or blocks of houses built for them by their employers. Each house had a main living room, with smaller rooms leading off it and stairs up to the roof, which was often the coolest place in the house. The poorest people of all had to make do with one-room huts made of mud-brick, which they shared with their animals.

Similarly, the kinds of food and drink varied according to wealth. The rich ate and drank very well. They had servants who would grow and prepare food for them. The peasants' diet was, in contrast, very simple and consisted of bread, beer, dried meat, fish and vegetables.

The family was important to the Egyptians because they needed someone to tend their spirits when they died. Many paintings of the time show parents playing with their children, who seem to have had plenty of toys made of wood or leather. Egyptian families kept pets too.

Above *A chest from the tomb of Amenophis III. It is made of wood inlaid with blue glazed china. The hieroglyphics are gilded.*

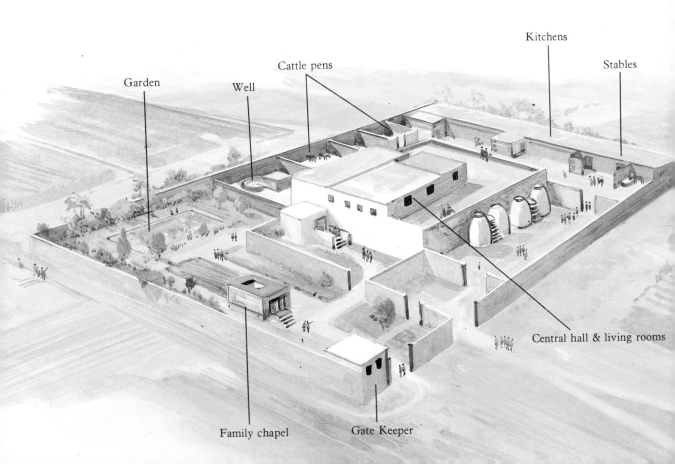

7 EXPANDING FRONTIERS

Trade and tribute

Although Egypt was rich in farmland and building stone, she relied on other countries to supply her with many of the goods she needed. If these could not be obtained through trading, they would be taken by force if necessary. The most obvious trading route was the Nile River itself. Great ships sailed down the river to the Mediterranean, and thence to Syria and Lebanon. We have already seen how vital the Lebanese cedars were to to treeless Egypt. Syria supplied silver, slaves and horses.

Whenever the power of Egypt weakened, these countries soon turned against her. Military expeditions were frequently sent there to subdue the people. During the New Kingdom, they were also made to pay tribute, as a sign that they had been conquered.

Merchant ships made the perilous voyage down the Red Sea to the Land of Punt. It is not clear exactly where Punt was, but it may have been part of present day Somalia. Here they bought gold and scented resins, such as myrrh and incense, which the Egyptians valued highly. Eventually an overland route was opened to the coast along the Wadi Hammamat, which made the journey shorter. In fact, most trade came overland. Mining expeditions, escorted by soldiers, traveled to Sinai to dig for copper and turquoise. Caravans came north from Africa, bearing ebony, ivory, leopard skins, ostrich feathers and many other exotic things. The gold to pay for all this came from Nubia, which successive Pharaohs struggled to keep under control.

In 1450 B.C. the Egyptian empire included Nubia and Syria (see inset map). Throughout Egypt's history she relied on the surrounding countries to supply her with certain goods. These countries were often hostile but safe trade routes were set up overland eventually.

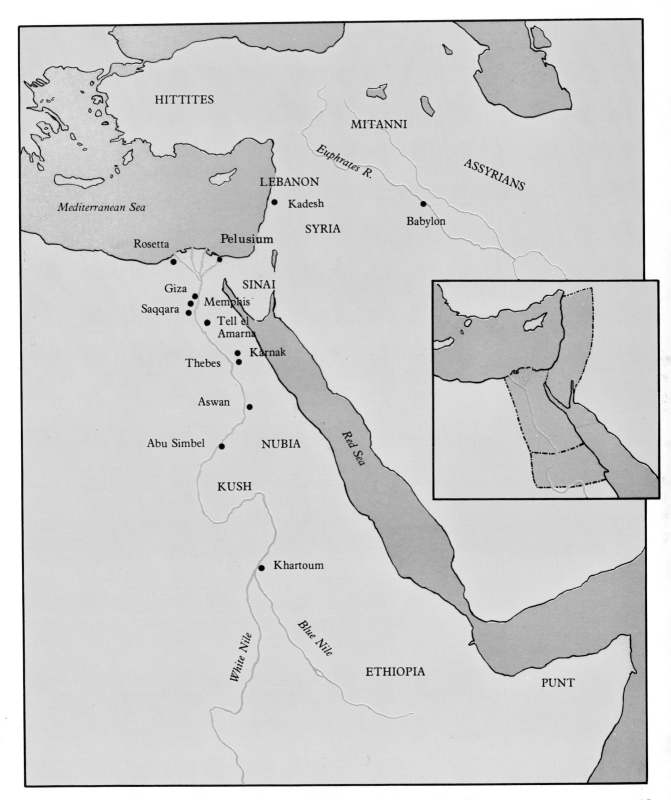

Going to war

The Egyptians' success at regaining lost territories, such as Nubia, was due to the fact that they learned to use the horse and chariot from the Hyksos.

Below *Rameses II was a great warrior Pharaoh.*

For many centuries, Egypt was so isolated that there was no need for a large standing army. Whenever troops were needed for expeditions to punish, say, the Nubians or Libyans, they would be levied from each of the nomes or provinces. The shock of invasion by the Hyksos brought a new warlike spirit to the country. The Egyptians had to learn how to defeat their attackers, how to expand their

frontiers and how to keep neighboring states under control. To accomplish this, they swiftly built up an efficient and well-equipped army.

By tradition, their military leader was the Pharaoh. Some were more heroic than others, but most of them did lead their armies into battle. Rameses II was shown in many paintings as a great warrior, defeating the Hittite army single-handedly.

The introduction of the chariot, from the Hyksos, had a dramatic effect upon Egyptian warfare. While a charioteer drove, a soldier behind would fire arrows at the enemy. The chariots were backed up by foot soldiers carrying spears, battleaxes or bronze swords.

In later years an Egyptian navy was also developed to deal with attacks from the Sea Peoples of the Mediterranean. In a great battle at the mouth of the Nile, Ramses III was victorious when his ships rammed the enemy's boats and sank them.

In the centuries after the death of Rameses III, Egypt was invaded by the Libyans, Nubians, Assyrians, Babylonians and Persians until the arrival of Alexander the Great in 332 B.C.

8 THE DECLINE OF THE EMPIRE

Invaders!

Rameses III was the last of the great Egyptian kings. His reign ended in turmoil in 1158 B.C. when he may have been assassinated. Gradually, Egypt lost her territories in Asia. There were fewer expeditions to mine for copper, and less gold to trade with. Tomb robbers broke into the royal tombs at Thebes and stole the hidden riches.

In the centuries that followed, several attempts were made to restore the country's pride, but all were swamped in a series of invasions. First a Libyan dynasty established itself at Bubastis, on the Nile Delta. Then, after a period of civil war, kings from Nubia took control of Thebes and Memphis. But there were far greater forces yet to contend with. In the seventh century B.C. the Assyrians were angered when Egypt joined a campaign against them. They advanced into the country and destroyed the Egyptian army in 663 B.C., sacking the city of Thebes and looting its great treasures.

The Assyrians were followed by the Babylonians, who did not bother to occupy Egypt but appointed their own ruler. They in turn were eclipsed by the Persians, who won a decisive victory at Pelusium in 525 B.C. Finally, in 332 B.C., the invincible Macedonian army of Alexander the Great arrived at the gates of Memphis and the Persians surrendered without a fight.

Egyptian soldiers used many different weapons.
1 Bow. 2 Scimitar. 3 & 4 Battle-axes. 5 Dagger. 6 Sword.
They also carried spears and shields. Their uniform was made of leather covered with metal scales.

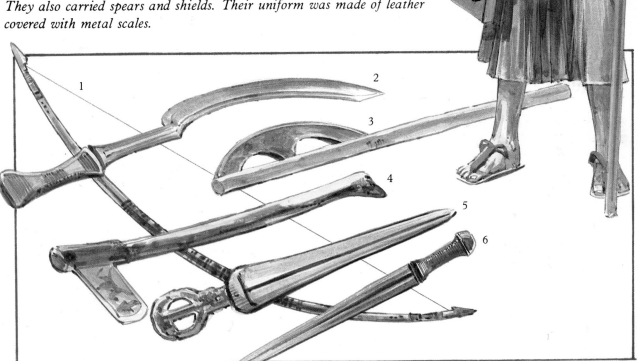

A province of Rome

Alexander was welcomed as the deliverer of Egypt from Persian bondage. He made sacrifices to the Egyptian gods, and was swiftly accepted as the new Pharaoh. Before he died, only nine years later, he founded the port of Alexandria to the west of the Nile Delta.

The kingdom of Egypt was entrusted to the son of one of Alexander's commanders, Ptolemy I. His line ruled for three centuries, but they often had to employ large numbers of Macedonian troops to keep the peace. In the end, Egypt became part of the young Roman Empire of Octavian Caesar, who later changed his name to Augustus.

The Romans shipped grain from Egypt back to Rome to feed their people.

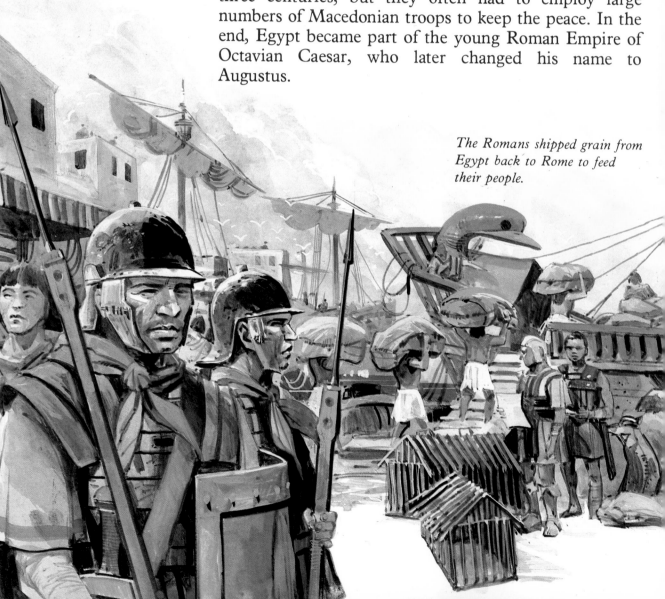

The Romans regarded their new prize as a rich land to be squeezed dry. With typical efficiency, they cleared out the irrigation ditches which had been neglected by the Ptolemies. The huge grain crops of the Nile Valley were needed to feed the people of Rome, and the Egyptians had what was left. The Roman system of taxation was even harsher than that of the old Pharaohs. Although the Emperor Tiberius once told a controller "You should shear my sheep, not skin them," the Egyptian natives grew steadily poorer.

The final blow fell in A.D. 383, when the Emperor Theodosius ordered that all pagan (non-Christian) temples should be closed down. The statues of the gods were torn from their sanctuaries and chopped to pieces. The civilization of the ancient Egyptians died along with their religion.

Above *In the fourth century A.D., the Roman Emperor ordered the destruction of all statues of Egyptian gods.*

Below *Ptolemy I.*

Above *Howard Carter found the tomb of the young Pharaoh, Tutankhamun, after years of searching.*

Below *The Rosetta stone.*

9 REDISCOVERY OF AN ANCIENT CIVILIZATION

The tomb of Tutankhamun

Over the centuries, the ruins of this ancient and forgotten civilization were pillaged. Temples were pulled down so that the stone could be used for building houses, and tombs and palaces were plundered.

In the late eighteenth century the discovery which thrilled the world was made by a French soldier. During the building of a fort near Alexandria he dug up a stone slab covered with the writing of two ancient languages, Egyptian and Greek. By that time, people had learned to read ancient Greek. This made possible the first translation of Egyptian hieroglyphics. By the middle of the nineteenth century, the Egyptian government at last realized what fabulous treasures it possessed. A Frenchman, Auguste Mariette, was put in charge of all excavations. He soon stopped the wholesale pillaging of ancient sites, and established the first Egyptian museum, housed today in Cairo.

At the beginning of this century an archaeologist named Howard Carter painstakingly searched the Valley of the Kings in the hope of finding a tomb that had not been broken into. At last in 1922, he came upon a step cut in the rock that led down to a door bearing the seal of the Pharaoh Tutankhamun. The tomb was opened and the most astounding collection of riches was found. It was, in fact, the most valuable archaeological find ever made and caused a sensation throughout the world. When Carter's patron, Lord Carnavon, died a few months later, the press invented a Pharaoh's curse to account for his death.

Below left *The funeral mask, from Tutankhamun's tomb, which was placed over the young king's face.*

Below right *Mary eleborate jewels were found in the tomb.*

10 THE EGYPTIAN LEGACY

When Christianity was swept away by the Muslim conquest of Northern Africa in A.D. 642, Egypt entered a period of over a thousand years of isolation. Her strength and her influence were all but forgotten. As we have seen the riches of this ancient civilization were gradually rediscovered.

During the 3,000 years spanned by the Egyptian civilization — from the first Pharaoh until the death of Cleopatra in 30 B.C. — their daily life, language, religion, and art scarcely changed. The most amazing fact about this civilization is that so much has survived to this day.

The written records, art and artifacts have remained inside the pyramids and the many tombs. As we have seen, the paper the scribes wrote on was made from papyrus reed. This was the first kind of paper ever manufactured.

In the area of medical science the Egyptians were very advanced. As early as the Old Kingdom, they had established a scientific means of medical analysis. They produced the first medical books, which gave instructions in surgery, the use of bandages, sutures and splints.

They explored arithmetic, engineering, astronomy, and botany. They had sundials and waterclocks to tell the time of day, and tables of the stars to tell the time at night. As early as 3000 B.C. they had developed a calendar of 365 days, divided into twelve months.

Huge monuments still stand as demonstrations of their advanced skills in architecture and engineering. The great pyramid of Cheops, which dominates the desert plateau at Giza, is perhaps the most astounding. It remains one of the most remarkable buildings ever erected.

Right *Part of a papyrus; a painted relief from the tomb of the Pharaoh Seti I; a water clock; Cleopatra's needle in London; the pyramids of Ancient Egypt.*

Table of dates

B.C.

3200 Narmer unites Upper and Lower Egypt and becomes the first ruler.

3120-2686 Early Dynastic Period — Dynasties 1 and 2.

2686-2180 The Old Kingdom — Dynasties 3-6.

2650 The Step Pyramid is built at Saqqara for King Zoser.

2575 The Great Pyramid is built at Giza.

2180-2133 First Intermediate Period — Dynasties 7-10 unrest and famine.

2133-1633 The Middle Kingdom. Established first of all by the Theban princes — Dynasties 11-13.

1633-1567 Second Intermediate Period Dynasties 14-17. Lower Egypt invaded by Hyksos from Asia, who are eventually driven out by Theban forces.

1567-1085 The New Kingdom — Dynasties 18-20.

1490 Queen Hatshepsut becomes the first woman to rule Egypt. Tuthmosis I is the first Pharaoh to be buried in the Valley of the Kings.

1450 Tuthmosis III reaches the Euphrates River, and subdues Palestine and Syria: the greatest extent of Egyptian power.

1367 Akhenaten breaks with old religions and builds new capital at Tell el Amarna.

1350 Tutankhamun reigns for a few years; his tomb not reopened until 1922.

1286 Rameses II narrowly avoids defeat at the Battle of Kadesh.

1218 First attacks by the Sea Peoples repelled.

1182 Rameses III defeats the Sea Peoples on land and at sea.

1085-656 Third Intermediate Period — Dynasties 21-25. Power is seized first by Libyans and then by Nubians.

663 The Assyrians plunder Thebes and leave their own appointee on the throne.

656-332 The Late Period — Dynasties 26-30.

605 Egyptian army utterly defeated by the Babylonians at Carchemish.

525 After the battle of Pelusium, the Persians under Cambyses conquer Egypt.

332 Alexander the Great and his Macedonian troops defeat the Persians; Alexander becomes Pharaoh.

332-30 The Ptolemaic Period. Increasing number of Greeks arrive.

69 Cleopatra, last queen of Egypt, is born.

48 Julius Caesar arrives in Egypt in pursuit of Pompey.

31 Battle of Actium: Cleopatra and Mark Antony defeated by Octavian. Egypt becomes a Roman province.

A.D.

383 All pagan temples closed down in favor of Christianity.

642 Muslim invasion of North Africa.

Glossary

Alabaster A fine-grained type of limestone greatly loved by the Egyptians for the carving of vessels and statues.

Assyrians The peoples whose great empire included modern-day Syria, Turkey and Iraq, and whose constant attacks brought about the decline of Egypt.

Delta The area of land created by a river's depositing silt at the point where it enters the sea.

Dynasty A line of rulers who inherit the throne for each other.

Hieroglyphs A picture, or symbol, which stands for a word or sound.

Hittites The peoples of present-day Turkey and Syria who challenged Egyptian power during the New Kingdom.

Hyksos A race of desert nomads from Asia who infiltrated Egypt and took control after the decline of the Middle Kingdom.

Nilometer A gauge, consisting of a series of marks cut in a rock, to show when and how fast the Nile River was rising.

Nomarch One of the provincial governors of Egypt, in charge of a nome.

Obelisk A tall and tapering shaft of stone, often carved to record the deeds of a great person.

Papyrus A type of reed growing near the Nile, which was used to make paper.

Pharaoh In Egyptian, "The Great House" — the respectful way of referring to the king without using his name.

Punt An ancient country on the shores of the Red Sea, possibly modern-day Somalia, which supplied Egypt with myrrh and other riches.

Sea Peoples A group of different races, including the Philistines, who attacked Egypt during the thirteenth century B.C.

Sphinx A statue of a lion with a man's head: the most famous of these is at Giza near the Great Pyramid.

Triumvirate The three ruling officials of the Roman Empire.

Books to read

Asimov, Isaac. *Egyptians*. Boston: Houghton Mifflin, 1967.

Ferguson, Sheila. *Growing Up in Ancient Egypt*. North Pomfret, VT: David & Charles, 1980.

Burland, Cottie A. *Ancient Egypt*. Chester Springs, PA: Dufour Editions, 1974.

Glubok, Shirley, ed. *Discovering Tut-Ankh-Amen's Tomb*. New York: Macmillan, 1968.

Glubok, Shirley and Tamarin, Alfred. *The Mummy of Ramose*. New York: Harper & Row, 1978.

Macaulay, David. *Pyramid*. Boston: Houghton Mifflin, 1975.

Millard, Anne. *Ancient Egypt*. New York: Franklin Watts, 1979.

Payne, Elizabeth. *The Pharaohs of Ancient Egypt*. New York: Random House, 1981.

Peach, L. Dugarde. *Cleopatra and Ancient Egypt*. Bedford Hills, NY: Merry Thoughts.

Purdy, Susan and Sandak, Cass R. *Ancient Egypt*. New York: Franklin Watts, 1982.

Streatfield, Noel. *The Boy Pharaoh*. Bridgeport, CT: Merrimack Publishing Corp., 1972.

Index

Picture Acknowledgments

The illustrations in this book were supplied by: courtesy of the Ashmolean Museum 19; courtesy of the Trustees of the British Museum 23, 28, 29, 30, 37, 50; The Mansell Collection 8, 9, 17, 23 (top), 25, 33, 36, 38, 44, 53; The Radio Times Hulton Picture Library 24, 41; R. Minall 53.